Kids
Africa in Childhood Poetry

Munyaradzi Mawere

Langaa Research & Publishing CIG
Mankon, Bamenda

Publisher
Langaa RPCIG
Langaa Research & Publishing Common Initiative Group
P.O. Box 902 Mankon
Bamenda
North West Region
Cameroon
Langaagrp@gmail.com
www.langaa-rpcig.net

Distributed in and outside N. America by African Books Collective
orders@africanbookscollective.com
www.africanbookcollective.com

ISBN: 9956-791-65-2

© Munyaradzi Mawere 2014

DISCLAIMER
All views expressed in this publication are those of the author and do
not necessarily reflect the views of Langaa RPCIG.

Dedication

To the children of Africa and beyond!

Table of Contents

She Deserves a Good Life Too

Father
Mother
Brother
Sister
I deserve a good life
To be loved
To be embraced
To be rewarded
To be smiled at
To be cared for
To be shown that I am worth

When going to school
To work up early in the morning
In clean uniforms
Armed with everything that keep my day alive
Books
Breakfast
And lunch

Yesterday
I felt for her
That girl
The orphan lonely girl
Tembi

Denied love at home
With scruffy hair and tattered uniforms

At school they refuse to share with her
I saw her lips dry
The angst timbre on her face
Vexed
Lonely she was seated
Outside at break time

I felt for pitiable Tembi
I befriended her
To share my love with her
To share my food with her
To smile at her as we talk
To show her that she is worth loving
For like me
She deserves a good life

Life of a Chameleon

How I am born
Depends
On whom my father is

I am a specialized clad of lizard
Thin and long
But indeed specialized

My clothes!
I change a hundred times a day
When I am not safe
I camouflage away
When I want to prey
I camouflage away
When I want to change my body temperature
I camouflage away
When I want to attract potential mates
I camouflage away
All my life I blend into backgrounds

My tongue!
A long, living magnet
That snatches from a distant
Yes
I am chameleon
The territorial lizard
The busking lizard
The specialized clad of lizard

A Letter to My Father

My heart breaks
My heart bleeds
Releasing gastric tears down my stomach
Crying for you father
Not because I hate you
But because I love you

I wish you spend some time with us father
Your own blood
Your own flesh
Watching us growing up
Embracing us in your lovely hands
Teaching us good morals
Teaching us that we are worthy children
Teaching us how to play the games you grew up playing
with your friends

But look father
You are always busy
Racing to acquire the fortunes of this world
You say for you and us
Fine
And you say you care for us
But only materially
My only questions:
'When shall you attend to our emotional needs?
When shall you attend to our psychological needs?'

We are growing up
Only dreaming of your face
For you go when we are still asleep
And come back when we have gone to bed

My Brother and the Mirror

I wish he could understand the way I do
That he who is in the mirror will never come out
Walk and play around with him as he wishes

Image in the mirror will never turn into a real person
It will stay forever an image

But my little brother!
He spends lots of time
Constantly staring
Smiling
Sometimes shouting
Calling at him who is in the mirror

I listen
The clicks he makes sound like he's saying
'Hey you little boy come out and let us run after one
another'

Guest of Honor

The night mosquitoes are throwing a party tonight
After a windy cold day yesterday
They are inviting you guys to attend

They are deadly hungry
They can't miss the party
Especially a party with juice
But only with at least one guest of honor from you guys
Otherwise the party will be postponed

If you are kind enough to cause their great delight
Just turn up for the party
It will be convened in that old room without
windowpanes
Room number 55

Don't take your blanket
You will not be allowed to sleep
Not even a single minute
Please don't miss it
You will be the guest of honor
Beware!

Take it Slow

To begin with
I want to learn about you before anything
Before I dance to your song
Before we travel in the same train
Your hand on my shoulder
My hand on your waist

We should take it slow
The chameleon way
Careful with each other's step
Beginning to get a little closer
Lost in the charming music
Only for a while

We should take it slow
Never allow our eyes closed
To see the real in each other
As we spin through the passage of time
Waiting
For the blessings that the future hold for us
Be it granted

Son of Long Street

Born of a mother
Born of a father
Free and happy
But only for a moment
Brief

Now I am alone
In the midst of Long Street
Who took me here, I don't know
Where they took me from, I don't know

I live by myself
A father and mother to myself
No shelter
No clothes
No food
My water, sour tears of my eyes
Hunger and thirsty my friends
Greet me day and night
But with harsh words

I envy those little once of my age
Crossing Long Street guided
Cared for by their mothers
When I am neglected by everyone who passes by
Even the priests and pastors
Educators and governors

I am so lonely
No one cares
The people
The government
They make fun of me

I watch them as they pass by
Cheering past
Laughing hysterically past
Making noises of joy
They don't care

Educated they appear to be
But their thinking lower than mine
The never gone to school

When they look at me
They shake their heads
Thinking I am the source of my own vexation
Even when they talk justice
They only talk about their own justice
Their constitution reads not my name
For in their domain I exist not
Me
Son of Long Street

Teenager Prayer for Mom and Father

Thank you mom
Thank you father
For introducing me to this world
A world I never knew
A world I never imagined

Mom
Your touching love
I will never forget
Feeding me out of your own juice
Washing my stench naps with open noses
Bathing my dirty body with soft hands

Father
Your wonderful care
I will never forget
You never let me starve
You never let me sent away from school for fees arrears
You preferred to put on faded trousers for my sake
That I sleep on a comfortable bed

Mom
Father
Your great love
I will never forget

I pray therefore
That the Lord God

Grant your long life
That the Lord God
Bless you even more
Forever and ever
Amen!

Where Do I Belong?

Please teach me
Please teach
I don't understand
When in class
They divide us into two groups
Boys and girls

Even in official documents
Birth certificates
There are these labels
Male
Or
Female

In sports at school
They do the same
Boys' marathon!
Girls' marathon!

I am in between
Neither a girl
Nor
A boy
I am not represented
Where do I belong?

Termites

If anything inspires
Termites inspire even a fool
If people work hard
Termites work even harder
Worse still in the absence of foremen

Tiny in size
They are wiser than Mr gigantic elephant

Termites
They know seasons more than poor farmers
They know when to prepare
They know when to gather
They know when to harvest

From dawn to dusk
They are busy
Up and down the whole forest
They line up one by one
To fill their granaries
In preparedness for tomorrow
For they know future is night
Go now
Go!
Go and learn from them
Free teachers

Slaves of Habits

Slavery has gone but present
In many
Even today
It persists
They are all slaves

Tedy spends all day on television
He is slave to television

Doro spends all day drinking
He is slave to beer

Weed spends all day smoking
He is slave to drugs

Rudo spends all day thinking about her boyfriend
She is slave to love

Tabantu and Tundra spend all day gossiping
They are slaves to gossip

They all think they are free
Never
They are all slaves of habits
For they indulge in bad habits

Our Old Cock

When he was a chick
He flew together with the flock
Scratching the ground all day
With all family near

Days have gone
Things have changed
He no longer walks with the family
He is now clock of the village
A specialist of time

At twelve midnight
He crows
A signal of the approaching day
At four in the morning
He crows
A signal of the approaching sun
At six
He crows
A signal of the rising sun

At times
I see him on one leg
His head in his wing
His mind casting back
To the old days
When he flew together with family
Now he knows
His days are numbered

A Friend Indeed

I learnt from my teacher
That a friend in need is a friend indeed
Now I know who my friend is

My real friend
He who loves me when in trouble
He who visits me when ill
He who advices when fooling myself on forged
imaginations
He who cares for me when in tribulation
He who takes me up by hand when fall
He who offers me shelter when raining outside
He who offers me food when hunger gnaws
He whose feelings never fade
He who shares with me in the long journey of life
He who when I take a sweet out of his mouth does not
cry
He who understands my situation
So,
My teacher was right when he taught
That a friend in need is a friend indeed

Rose My Flower

You are perennial
A friend always available
You are resilient
A friend that teaches courage
A palace of beauty
Rose the virtuous

You sit there all year long
When your neighbours go to bed
You stay watching the night
When harsh weathers approach
You stand to face the challenge
Even when gusty winds promise
You are resilient

Resilience and beauty
Virtues that rarely match
Only in you they reconcile
Your pink soft petals
Bright and sweet
You are friend to everyone
Even to Mr B
Our ever busy friend

The Sun's Journey

He is never tired
His journey is endless
Swerakuenda
You see him everyday
Coming from the east
He never misses his way
To the west
He goes

This man
Round!
He seem to determine our actions
When he comes from the east
We wake up, going out to play
When he sinks into the western mountains
We wave each other goodbye
Leaving behind our plastic balls
And the grounds
All unattended

But one is one day
We will make an attempt
Plead with him
That he stops for a while
There on midday
That we enjoy our game

The Story of My Teacher

She told me one day
A thrilling incredible story
That those trees we see
Big and small
Grew up from seeds
Cared and provided with right conditions by their mother
nature
As we see with budding flowers
That today they are buds
Tomorrow they are flowers
Bright and beautiful

She never ceased to amaze me
With her story she went on
To tell us all in our class
That she was once a child
A little baby
Cared for and loved by her own mother
Provided with everything she needed
She was educated
That today she educates us

Ummm!
But she told me one more thing
That among those flowers
Some smell sweet
Others are sour
I cried!
That I grow up a sweet flower

Harare

Umm!
What is with this name?
Harare!

My name my mother told me
That I am Tinashe
God is with us
My brother's name my mother told me
That he is Takomborerwa
We have been blessed
And my sister's name my mother told me
That she is Tadiwa
We are loved

Now Harare!
What is with this name?
I am puzzled
I want to go to Harare
To discover for myself
What is with that name
Harare

That Old Boy

In my classroom is all beauty
The charts
The chalkboard
Our science corner
And my friends
They are all nice

When I look at my friends
They have really big smiles on their faces
And me
I do
They wrong you
They say sorry
And me
I do

Only that old boy
A problem
You get more marks than him
You are in trouble
You don't share your food with him
You are in trouble
You joke with him that he is father of the class
You are in trouble
He wrongs you
He laughs

That old boy!
He is bully
He makes my heart heavy
But one day is one day
I will report him to my teacher

A Good Student

My teacher once asked us all
Simple but educative questions:

Would a good student make noise when in class
Playing when it is time to study?

My friend does

Would a good student sleep
Deliberately forgetting to do homework
Homework that should be marked next morning?

My friend does

Would a good student talk bad about his teacher
Gossiping that teacher so and so is bad because she
always give us homework
And insist on marking the work next morning?

My friend does

Would a good student always come late to school
Arriving two hours after lessons started?

My friend does

Would a good a student never apologies

Whenever done something wrong to his peers or teacher in class?

My friend does
So he is not a good student

My Last Pain

I go for a day or so with an empty stomach
Nobody notices
I go to school with dirty, tattered uniforms
Nobody is bothered

I desperately beg for help
Nobody hears my little voice
I even beg in a louder cry
They say 'leave him he is mad'
I sit lonely with frail dry lips
They say 'don't talk to him he is crazy'
I hang my head down
They say 'look at him he is wild'
The face of my mom
I know not
For she died when I was only one
To deprive me of all love
Dispossessed

All my hope they have taken away
All my battles they have worn
All my joys they have scattered
All my happiness they have stolen
To create in me a dejected teen

Now my spirit is weary
My body is exhausted
Still nobody cares for the two

At last
They decide to part ways
Spirit his own way
Body to the mortuary
That's when those who appear to care
Only get preoccupied
But I have gone for good
Elsewhere
In desperate pain

Taramanda

My dear friend Taramanda
Someone out there called here
It was night
Midnight
She answered the call
She went
Hoping she will be back soon
But it's a decade now
Since she went
After promising me
With a fading voice
'Stay here
I will come back soon
I am being summoned...'

Child Soldiers

It is horror that I see in Africa and beyond
In Iraq
And Afghanistan
Incredible recipe of all disasters
The unimaginable
The unthinkable

Child soldiers
In their teens I see
With AK 47 on their shoulders
They know what it means to kill
They are even thirsty for human blood

Child soldiers
They fight fiercely all day long
Their bodies under the influence of deadly *suruma* drug
They burn houses like they burn grass in the forest
They kill people like they slaughter chicken on a wedding
day

Ask them one question:
'What are you fighting for?'
They know not what
For they never learnt what peace is all about

Their upbringing was misguided
By abject imbecility flaunted in falsity and treachery
They never learnt what it means to love others

They never learnt what it means to do justice
Their minds too young to understand they are being used
I blame the elders

Child soldiers
Their task they execute without questioning
They fight without asking why
They kill without asking why
They burn without asking why
For their minds are too young to understand the perils of
war
I protest
On behalf of my brothers and sisters in war

Gifts Taken for Granted

There are too many gifts in this world
Taken for granted by many
The first to be born alive in this world
Many others follow
Love from our parents and the world we are given for free
The sun that rises and sets to help us plan our activities
The moon that shines at night when dark should conquer
The rain that nourishes the earth when plants and soil are thirsty
The air that presents itself even to beggars that we breathe to move on with life
The water that never complain even when we wash in it our dirty clothes
The ground that never protest even if we dance on it everyday
The fruits of the forest that we eat without them asking us to be eaten in turn
The sunshine that we enjoy without it asking us for rentals
All these and others, you name them
Are gifts that we take for granted

The Purpose of Life

When I was growing up
I think at 9
Puzzled by the purpose of life we live
I once asked my mother
'Mother what is the purpose of our life?'
For my friend had told me
'The purpose of our life is to eat, drink, and sleep'
I had also read from the newspaper
'That the purpose of life is to work and become rich'
And I wanted to hear from the most trusted person ever
My mother
She was puzzled too
For she never expected a question of that magnitude

Scratching her head
She sent me for plates outside the kitchen
My mind stolen by the sweet smell of her delicious dish
I forgot to pursue

Moments later
We parted ways

I have not ceased searching
All this time I have been hunting for it
Now I know
Truth
Goodness
And above all, Love

Dear Teacher

Teacher!
To this world I came
True
With my appearance as it is
With my skin color as it is
With my family background as it is
With my look as it is
With my persona as it is

Teacher!
I have watched you a hundred times
I beg you
Judge me not by my color
Judge me not by my appearance
Judge me not by my family background
For that will be unfair

Teacher!
I beg you
Look at my work not me
Judge my ability and not my poverty
Discuss my school work to help and not my family
background
For that will be unfair

Teacher!
All I need from you is proper guidance
To read

To write
To understand
To excel
And to lead by example
Thank you!

Teach me Good

I see you BIG
I see a role model
I see kindness
I see love
I see joy
I see peace
I see help
I see smile
I see respect
I see welcome
I see good
I come for your embrace
Teach me kindness
Teach me love
Teach me no spite
Teach me no murder
Teach me no brutality
Teach me no difference
Teach me no detestation
Teach me no hate speech
Teach me no gossip
Teach me no corruption
Teach me no deceit
Teach me no cruelty
Teach me no war
Teach me no damage
Teach me all good
For I deserve to be good

Naughty Little Kids

Once feeding
We are full of energy
Just put us in our own class
You will see what we are really made of
Naughty little kids
Fun in everything
Sometimes strange

We like so much running after each other
We like so much talking at the top of our voices
We like so much fun food fighting
We like so much asking too many questions
We like so much playing fun tricks
We like so much experimenting on anything that comes
to mind
We like so much understanding everything but we have
no patience to concentrate

You call us naughty little kids
Don't hurt us
Teach us
This is our nature
You also walked through the same road

Sister Lily

Sister Lily I admire you
When you wash plates clean like winter moonlight
Teach me I think I could do it

Sister Lily I admire you
When you balance a clay pot full of water on your head
Teach me I think I could do it

Sister Lily I admire you
When you balance a bottle full of sand in a race
Teach me I think I could do it

Sister Lily I admire you
When you knit your little jerseys with used wool
Teach me I think I could do it

Sister Lily I admire you
When you play *bata musoro*
Teach me I think I could do it

Sister Lily I admire you
When you skip high in *fishu-fishu*
Teach me I think I could do it

Sister Lily I admire you
When you play *pada*
Teach me I think I could do it

Sister Lily I admire you
When you write your name in the sand
Teach me I think I could do it

Lead Them by Example

What we teach them speak for themselves
What we show them reveal for themselves
What we share with them manifest for themselves

We share with them Godly love
Their works will tell
We teach them hard work
Their results will speak
We share with them bad things
Their actions will speak

For the sake of their future
Their goodness
Show them the right way
Teach them the right things
And lead them by example

Playing with Summer

Winter has come
To take away our happiness
To dress our faces with masks of sadness
To fill our hearts with bitterness

We go to school barefooted
There are small stones with biting teeth on that hill path
Waiting eagerly to bite our feet
We are never friends

In the sky
The sun has changed its mood
It used to be our good friend but nowadays
Ah!
Winter stole away his good heart

We look forward for summer
The best friend of sun
That the sun shines
That we step out and play free outside
Enjoying the coolness of the breeze that summer winds
bring
Enjoying the nourishment of the life that summer rains
bring
That day
We will step out and play with summer

King of the Road

You command all
Like a commander in the army

You are obeyed by all road users
For all the power of the road is vested in you
To control all who use the road
Humans and vehicles

Everyone listens to you
When you speak by your face
For your power is vested in your face
Check the traffic now

When you turn your face red
All the traffic on the road stop
Waiting for your next command
Even the people know
They cannot cross over to the other side

When you turn your face amber
All the traffic on the road get ready, carefully
Ready to take off

When you turn your face green
All the traffic on the road know you have conceded
They can go
No harm
Even the people know

They can now cross over to the other side

Those who rebel against you
They know a heavy fine they will pay
Either by accident
Or through the king's boys
Boys!
They will catch up with the culprit
Rebel

Counting

My sister Rudo
Taught me how to count
To count up to twenty
Hear now my count:
One
Two
Three
Four
Five
Six
Seven
Eight
Nine
Ten
Eleven
Twelve
Thirteen
Fourteen
Fifteen
Sixteen
Seventeen
Eighteen
Nineteen
Twenty

Luminary

Luminary, teacher said I am
That sends my blood running fast all over the body
Bracing me for whatever competition ahead of time

With my teacher's call
I am ready for the race
Bound to win all my competitors
Because my teacher called me luminary

I will work out the most difficult mathematical problem
Representing my class in inter-class competitions
Representing my school in inter-district competitions
Representing my province in provincial competitions
Representing my province in national competitions
Because my teacher called me a luminary

I will write a poem
A poem that will speak to all children
Teaching them to work hard
Teaching them to pursue truth
Teaching them to be just
Teaching them to be exemplary
Because my teacher called me luminary

I will play chess today
Come what may
I will say check mate to my contestant
Because my teacher called luminary
And I feel like a luminary

Fruit Trees in my Village

I look east
I see a cape fig tree
I look west
I see a bird plum tree
I look south
I see a wild loquat tree
I look north
I see a waterburry tree

He looks east
He sees a sweet monkey orange tree
He looks west
He sees a lippie tree
He looks south
He sees a baobab tree
He looks north
He sees a snot apple tree

She looks east
She sees a granite *garcinia* tree
She looks west
She sees a *batoka* plum tree
She looks south
She sees a *marula* tree
She looks north
She sees a snow berry tree

Anger

Anger is like cyclone eline
That sweeps away all happiness
It is an electric shock wave
That runs swiftly all over your body
Mad
And determined to hurt

It comes to replace joy
When heart is saddened
And reason is suspended

Its shocks!
Too overwhelming to master
They trigger fights
They break friendship
They send away reason
Warning him not to come back too soon

I wish reason refuses
To listen even a single minute
To all the commands of anger

Teru is Turning Six

Happy birthday to you Teru
Last year you were five
This year you are six
Next year you will be seven
Time moves

Last year you were in grade 1
This year you are in grade 2
Next year you will be in grade 3
Times moves
Let's sing together with time
For Teru our beloved friend:
Happy birthday Teru
Happy birthday to you
Happy birthday Teru
Happy birthday to you

Good Things to Good People

Are you nice
Presentable
Hospitable
Lovely
Generous
One
To whom
All goodness adheres?
If yes
Then I am so delighted
Because
I will give you a wonderful gift
That no one has ever received
Stay tune!

October Sun

I hate the October sun
Sun of the tropics

Inside house
Outside house
Under shade
Swimming in the river
It's all hot

I wish and dream
That I fly to another planet
Away far-away
Where I don't know
But where weather is cool
And where I can find sweet raindrops

I will come back when summer returns
To enjoy cool breeze from the south
And rainfall that gives us life
I hate the October sun

Green Poem

I love green things
I care for everything
That is green

The green plants around
I care for

At home
I care for the green lawn

In the garden
I care for the green vegetables

In the farmland
I care for the green crops

In the orchard
I care for the green fruit trees

In the plantation
I care for the green woodlot
Because I learnt green is life
And I love green

My Christmas Dream

On Christmas
My dream was to get a sparkling toy

I got a bicycle
But I didn't get a sparkling toy

I got a football
But I didn't get a sparkling toy

I got a doll
But I didn't get a sparkling toy

I got a packet of crayons
But I didn't get a sparkling toy

I got a new pair of trousers
But I didn't get a sparkling toy

I got a box of chocolate
But I didn't get a sparkling toy

Next Christmas
I hope dad and mom will buy me a sparkling toy

My Cat

My cat is lazy
Very lazy

Our house is full of rats
Rats that convene meetings even in the day light
Yet my cat is always hungry

She always waits desperately for me when at school
Only to cry *n'eu n'eu*
Whenever I am having my share

All she wants is my food
When inside the house lives her best food ever
Food that she can eat any time she feels hungry

Oh!
My cat is lazy
I don't want to be like my cat

Absent Minded

My body is here present
It is seated at a table
Food in its hand
But I am absent

Mom
I am sorry
I am not here to command the body to take in the food
He is waiting for my instruction
But I am not there
I am playing plastic balls in the pitch

Mom
I will come later
For now pardon me
I am absent

Parent's Prayer

May God the Almighty bless and keep you well always
May you grow up to be righteous
May you stand for truth always
May you strive to know the truth always
May all your good wishes be granted always
May you sing joy in your heart always
May you strive to do good for yourself and others always
May you aspire for success always
May you be courageous always
May you demonstrate unconditional love to others always
May you strive for justice to prevail for everyone always
May you be hard working always?
For hard work is always rewarded
Amen!

Nature

The world outside is amazing
Full of things that will never cease to amaze me

I look east
The sun is shining bright
Its dazzling rays feeding the rest of the earth

Around in the day
Birds of the earth are singing
Melodious songs they never trained in schools of music
Ku-u-kru-ku-u, ku-u-kru-ku-u
Tsvi-tsvo-ro-tsvi-tsvo-o
Sisi-i, sisi-i
Others are flying high in the sky
Demonstrating their God given air acrobatics

At night the joy continues
The moon is shining vividly
Accompanying the bull frogs of the waters
Frogs that sing hoarsely all night

From the south
Some warm breeze fills the air with embracing love
Promising to bring gentle rain that nurtures
With no lightning flashes, no thunder roars

Now the bees of the forest
Waiting anxiously for the flowers to bloom

That their sweet busy business may kick start

Also waiting happily are the trees
Their leaves drifting slowly all sides
Scratching their noses with the little finger

And animals of the forest
Only sing joy in different voices
As they wait for the rains
Once again to lubricate their throats

Lord Jesus

Wise men from the east
Great shepherds
The melodious singing of the angels
And the echoes of the pound of the angels' dances
They heard
As the angels rejoiced

Up in the sky they gazed
A dazzling shining star they saw
A sign of Him, light of earth and heaven

From heaven He descended
Humble and meek
To appear in the virgin's womb
That in the sty he could be born

But the wise men knew
He was not a human babe
For to them the word had spoken

Frankincense, myrrh and gold they took
To Him, the master of love
To Him, the bearer of peace and joy
To Him, the Saviour
Lord Jesus

The Flood

Our land is invaded
Dirty fierce waters run mad as he goes
Running over land
Wrecking anything that stands in his way

I see flood surrounding land with vermillion ooze
Raging stronger and stronger fearlessly
Leaves and sand are driven into captivity
Off to the sea they are taken
I hear the judge declaring
'Life imprisonment under water my prison guard'
Then a crescendo of sounds
And I hear them crying as they go down to sea
Sadly
To stay forever more

When he sings
His hoarse voice sends the animals mad to the mountains
Birds fly high into the sky
Fearing to be involved in the battle
Trees stand on their knees
Praying to the Most High
Reeds shiver all day and night
Trembling in fear

Then land reorganise his army
For a great battle against flood
And flood run back to the sea

With a speed of a ghost
To hide from the wrath of land
Until another day he comes out again

Her Love

Her love has no expiry date
It's all life guaranteed love
Which started well before I were born

When I was months in her womb
She listened and obeyed all my requests

When I was nine months old
I told her I want to go out from here
She obeyed
With a smile on her face
From day one to year one I cried for food
She fed me
With a smile on her face

At two she bought me a walker
Taught me how to walk and run
When I fell, she took me up
With a smile on her face

At three she bought me all food I liked
I ate and splashed the leftovers all over the floor
She collected
With a smile on her face

At four she bought me a bicycle
Taught me how to cycle
With a smile on her face

At four she sent me to pre-school
Holding my hand all way
With a smile on her face

Now I am five
She bought me a beautiful school uniform
My lunch she has packed in my bag
With a smile on her face
For her love has no expiry date

The Sky

Every day I look up in the sky
All what I see is blue
But many times clouds
Fluffy and ashy
All in different shapes

I look there
A woman holding a baby
There
A fierce lion with a big head
There
A bird flying
There
A man seated on a stool
There
A cock crowing

I heard your house if full of many things
Dust particles
Air
And sometimes you mix them
To bring us rain
Ah, sky!
You are very rich

Polymath

My name is Polymath, aged 8
I write poems, so I am a poet
I paint walls, so I am a painter
I play guitar, so I am a guitarist
I play piano at school, so I am a pianist
I play drama at school, so I am an actor
I drive toy cars, so I am a driver
I play football, so I am a footballer
I sing songs, so I am a singer
I write books, so I am an author
I solve very difficult mathematical problems, so I am a
mathematician
I speak many languages, so I a multi-linguist
I cook for mom and dad, so I am a cook
I run at school, so I am an athlete
I teach my young siblings at home, so I am a teacher
I am Polymath
Renaissance Personality
Multipotentialite
Mr Everything

Will all my Dreams Come True?

All people have dreams
Some dreams come true
Others are shattered by circumstances
Never
Never to be realised again

Mine are dreams of hope
Glowing hope
Still fresh in the forming mind
Reserved for time to come

Every day I dream
To meet someone whom I will love
And will love me
Unconditionally
For the rest of my life

Every day I dream
To live in a world
Loving and peaceful
For the rest of my life

Every day I dream
To live a long life
Happy
And prosperous

Every day I dream

To live in a world
Where diseases and death
Are powerless stings

Every day I dream
To live in a world
Full of green vegetation
And blooming flowers

My only question:
Will all my dreams come true?

Peanut Butter

Peanut butter is my favourite
I like it on my bread
Spreading
Before munching

My little brother Kudzi
Enjoys it too
He steals it from grandma
When she is outside
Cooking

Peanut butter is my favourite
Our cat enjoys it too
Even the rats at night
They come scratching my lips when asleep
Searching for peanut butter
That is already in my tummy

Peanut butter is my favourite
When I am asleep I dream
Crying after grandma
For a crumb of peanut butter
Only to wake up cross
When grandma says to me:
'You will get it from your toast!'

Death of a Friend

We used to laugh together
And cry together
What we talked about
We never cared
For one reason
Trust

We would play plastic balls
All day
And I would let you win
We would play *tsoro yemutatu*
All day
And you would let me win
For one reason
Love

I remember at Christmas
When we would have our food together
I stop and think of the things we shared
They are more than I can remember
And I know those memories will always stay the same

You never said goodbye
Because you knew I will be sad
But I will stop not
To look for you all over
Even if I guess
They have taken you far far-off

You only visit me once in a while
Smiling
As I see you coming
I slap myself when I wake up
Because I know you will have gone
To a country far-off
To visit me again another day
For you know I always miss you

Gwariro

Gwariro
Gwariro is our school
Mother and father

Gwariro
Gwariro is our school
Mother and father

Send your children
Mother and father
Yes
Send your children
Mother and father

Yes
That the learn to read and write
Yes
That they learn maths and science

Yes
That they learn singing and dancing

Yes
That they learn moral rectitude and sport

Yes
Send your children
Mother and father

Dare Not Continue

All day that rises
You beat me up
You laugh at me
You make fun of me
You tease me like a moron
Befuddling me in the day light

Let me tell you what
If you were a zebra
And I am a lion
I would eat you up
Munching up your pieces
As you watch
Alive
Or guess
If you were peanut butter
And I am the cat
I would eat you up
Clean
Till there is no longer any sign
Of you in the tin

So,
Dare not continue
With your old dreadful habits

My Dog

Spider
Spider!
Where are you?

I looked in the kennel
You are not there

Spider
Spider!
Where are you?

Mom
Mom
My dog is lost!

Oh
Mom
Mom
My dog is lost!

I looked in the kennel
She is not there

Mom
Mom
My dog is lost!

Oh

Spider
Spider!
Where are you?

Everwishing Word

I have checked my dictionary
There is one word
That always wishes
That people always live in togetherness
That people's relationships be sealed forever

I wish I could meet you
To share that everwishing word
That many take for granted
Yet the backbone of all relationships
Come!
Let's meet
That we share
And spread fast
To the world yonder
The everwishing word:
'LOVE'

Command of Nature

When the sun rises
Birds sing all joy

When the sun sets
All run indoors
To spend the night closed

When the moon shines
Children go out playing

When polar-ice caps melt to smithereens
The northern spring emerges from its slumber

When *munakamwe* hits the tropics
Summer comes
Farmers put their hoes on shoulders

When September comes down to the South
All trees bloom with flowers

Wonders of the world!
All through the command of nature

Love of the Arms

Love comes in many ways
Words
Actions
All in their many forms

This one here
Is love embedded in four arms
Love of the arms
That wrap tight around the waists of the two
To join them in one embrace
In a few seconds of happiness
Letting them feeling the blood of the two bodies
Running fast each other

Guess what it is
Guess!

Abortion

They do as if they fell from heaven
And not born
They behave as if their mothers had iron hearts
And were never loved

By their mothers
They were born
Loved
Cared
They were never disposed of

They follow the instincts of their mad feelings
To receive from all men
Day and night
Till they forget the sire master
They connive with false friends
To rid he who is innocent
To dump who she is blameless

The innocent cry when they turn their back
But their hearts are all stones
They feel no pity
They know no love

God forbid
And receive that innocent
Keep him well till the day they will follow
To answer all the questions on their own

Everything is Home

Everything is home for something
Provided
We go by the understanding
That home is anything
To live
To rest
And to play

Water is home for fish
Hive is home for bees
Kennel is home for dogs
Den is home for lions
Stable is home for horses
Hole is home for rodents
Web is home for spider
Nest is home for birds
Sty is home for pigs

I visited the caves
Something lives there
I visited the rocks
Something lives there
I visited the rubbish pits
Something lives there
I visited the air
Something lives there
I visited the trees
Something lives there

I visited............
And you name it

So, everything is home
At least for something

Two Sides of the Same Coin

Hate and love
Two of the many things that exist together
But never meet
They are like oil and water

Hate is everything that love is never be

Hate works against
Love works for

Hate is full of chaos and confusion
Love is full of tranquillity and serenity

Hate is a bitter, dull flower
Love is a sweet, bright flower

Hate is darker than a dozen nights
Love is brighter than a dozen day lights
Hate is hopelessness
Love is hope

Yet love and hate
Like forehead and back
Like hope and hopelessness
Like friend and enemy
They exist side by side
Without one
The other never exists

They are two sides of the same coin
Which side do you choose?

Dove

Ku-u kruu ku-u
Ku-u kruu ku-u
Ku-u kruu ku-u

Happy and peaceful
This is dove
Don't you know?